trail follows the stream gradient. Heat is usually the main obstacle.

A few seep springs are passed in lower Hualapai Canyon, but the first dependable water (use only in an emergency) is Havasu Creek, 6.5 miles (10.5 km) down the trail. It should be treated before drinking. The eight-mile (13-km) walk to Supai normally takes two and one-half to three hours, but this depends a great deal on the time of day, weather, and a hiker's physical condition. Add at least an hour for the return trip. The campground is located two miles (3 km) farther down the canyon between Havasu and Mooney falls.

## DAY HIKES

Due to the remote location of the trailhead and the long distance to the first source of water, day hikes are not recommended.

The wide expanse of upper Hualapai Canyon below Hualapai Hilltop on the Havasu Trail

## THE HAVASUPAI PEOPLE

Forebears of today's Havasupai people began settling along the Grand Canyon's south rim more than 800 years ago, possibly assimilating an earlier Pueblo-like group, the Cohonina, who had lived there since AD 700. The new migrants arrived from the west and called themselves—as they still do today—the Pai, a Yuman word meaning "people." These early Havasupai were one of fourteen regional Pai bands scattered across northwestern Arizona, with the Havasupai being the easternmost. Close ties with Hopi trading partners far to the east fostered Pueblo cultural traits among the Havasupai that distinguished them from other Pai groups.

During the summer, the Pai farmed in canyons with perennial streams, and in winter they hunted and gathered wild foods on the plateau. Life continued in this way for generations. But in the latter half of the nineteenth century, things began to change.

Tyava, Havasupai basketmaker, 1898

When cowboys moved onto the plateau with their cattle, and miners began staking claims in Havasu Canyon, tensions increased between the Indians and the newcomers. By 1866, open war broke out. The U.S. Army defeated the Hualapais (the soldiers lumped together all the Pai fighting bands under the Hualapai name) after a bitter three-year guerrilla war that ended in 1869. Cavalry officers who had fought both said they would rather fight five Apaches than one Hualapai.

In the aftermath, the U.S. army and government treated the Havasupai separately because they had not participated as a group in the fighting. This worked to their advantage when President Rutherford Hayes established the Havasupai Indian Reservation in 1880 on 38,000 acres (15,000 ha) of land bordering Havasu Creek. Two years later this was reduced to a little more than 500 acres (200 ha). And so things remained for nearly a century.

In the early 1970s the Havasupai Tribal Council mounted a vigorous campaign to have some of their traditional lands on the plateau returned to them. "We missed the land," testified Ethel Jack at the land claims hearings. "But the land suffered just as much without us. You see, we belong to the land." After a contentious political struggle, 185,000 acres (75,000 ha) were added to the reservation in 1975. An additional 95,000 acres (38,500 ha) of Grand Canyon National Park were reserved for traditional purposes. The bill stated that these lands "shall remain forever wild," and nothing should detract from their scenic values.

Today, many Havasupais try to live by the traditional concept of harmony with all life. They desire to preserve the natural beauty of their homeland and see themselves as being an inseparable part of the land. They believe that if their homeland is destroyed, so are they.

## HISTORY OF THE TRAIL

Father Francisco Garcés

When the earliest Spanish explorers made contact, Havasupais ranged from the Colorado River on the north to the San Francisco Peaks on the south, and from the far side of the Little Colorado River on the east to the Hualapai country on the west.

Father Francisco Garcés was the first European to leave a written description of a visit to Havasu Canyon. Garcés was a Spanish missionary based at San Xavier del Bac, near what is today Tucson. In 1776 he traveled with a few Indian guides across northern Arizona intent on discovering a route between Sonora and Santa Fe. Finding Havasupais warm and hospitable, he stayed with them many days.

The leader of the first American party to enter Havasu Canyon thought they would be the last. The expedition began on the Colorado River in 1857 under the command of Lieutenant Joseph Ives. The army had instructed him to proceed upriver as far as a boat could navigate. The stern-wheeler was going full-steam-ahead when it hit a submerged rock, throwing men overboard and wrecking the boat.

Having found the head of navigation the hard way, Ives abandoned ship and traveled overland to what he called "Big Cañon." There he followed a trail leading down into the "frightful abyss" of Havasu Canyon. In his official report, Ives grumbled about the region he had traversed. "After entering it," he wrote, "there is nothing to do but leave. Ours has been the first, and will doubtless be the last, party of whites to visit this profitless locality."

Ives, of course, was embarrassingly wrong. Since then, visitors to Grand Canyon National Park have numbered in the millions, and many thousands make their way each year to the isolated Havasupai Indian Reservation. Travel to Havasu Canyon has changed since Ives's time—for one thing you no longer have to crawl down the trail on your hands and knees.

Members of an archaeological expedition stand above the fields of Supai, circa 1924

## GEOLOGY ALONG THE TRAIL

The world from Hualapai Hilltop is a land of rock. Only the warm colors that come at both ends of the day soften the hard geologic lines. The more resistant limestones and sandstones form great escarpments, dropping hundreds of feet to the softer, slope-forming shales. The dominant landforms seen from the trailhead are the bold cliffs of buff-white Coconino Sandstone and the broad bench that forms the rim of the inner canyon. Often bare of vegetation, this bench is called the Esplanade.

From the rim to the bottom of the falls, erosion has exposed in the canyon walls the classic Grand Canyon series of rocks. The Kaibab Formation caps the rim followed by the Toroweap Formation; Coconino Sandstone; Hermit Formation; the Supai Group, including the Esplanade; and the great Redwall Limestone. Below these, the creek cuts through the Temple Butte Formation and into the Tonto Group. The varying hardness of limestone, sandstone, and shale gives the land its stepped profile—cliff, slope, bench—a geological theme repeated throughout the canyon.

Havasu Creek flows north following the trend of the Supai Monocline. This feature is a massive fold in the underlying rock layers where the same types of rock on the east side of the canyon lie one hundred feet (30 m) higher than those on the west.

For many it is a surprise to find blocks of limestone on the rim embedded with fossil sponges and brachiopod shells. Although once deposited in warm, shallow seas, they now lie scattered among cactus and yucca in a high desert more than a mile above sea level.

These fossils must have once puzzled the Havasupais, too. They have a legend of a great flood that swept across the land with a roar louder than a thousand Colorado Rivers. Water covered even the tallest mountains by the time the rains stopped. As the storm broke, the waters rushed to the sea, cutting through the plateau and forming the Grand Canyon. The legend coincides with the theory of fossils deposited beneath seawater.

The Supai Group in the upper reaches of the Havasu Trail

## ECOLOGY ALONG THE TRAIL

The higher portions of the trail pass through a desert environment containing plants such as narrowleaf yucca (*Yucca angustissima*), Utah agave (*Agave utahensis*), and squawbush (*Rhus trilobata*). Increased shade and more moisture in the lower canyon allow a different mix of vegetation. Where water seeps to the surface, the mood of the canyon changes. Not only do you smell water before you see it, you also feel it. The sudden change in humidity creates a pocket with its own microclimate.

Water in the desert makes a critical difference. Along Havasu Creek grow huge Fremont cottonwood trees (*Populus fremontii*). A single tree helps moderate the temperature by transpiring up to 350 gallons (1,325 L) of water into the air each day. Redbud (*Cercis occidentalis*), singleleaf ash (*Fraxinus anomala*), and canyon grape (*Vitis arizonica*) can also be found.

A short distance from the creek grow mesquite (*Prosopis glandulosa*) and catclaw acacia (*Acacia greggii*), Mormon tea (*Ephedra viridis*) and sacred datura (*Datura meteloides*), all typical of the desert region. The line between dry and wet is sharply drawn.

Lizards are one of the few types of ani-

Ringtails are rarely seen during the day, but you may run across one in the campground at night.

mals seen in the heat of the day. Being cold-blooded, a lizard takes its body temperature from the surrounding environment and will suffer heat prostration between 104 and 116°F (40°-47°C). This forces it to make frequent trips back into the shade to cool down. Snakes are even more heat-sensitive and will survive only a few minutes on the exposed ground at midday.

Cottonwood trees along Havasu Creek

Large mammals living in the region of Havasu Canyon include mule deer (*Odocoileus hemionus*) and desert bighorn sheep (*Ovis canadensis*). At night you may encounter a ringtail (*Bassariscus astutus*) or a woodrat (*Neotoma* sp.), and during the day you may spot a rock squirrel (*Spermophilus variegatus*) on a hunt for trail mix.

Birds commonly seen by hikers are the American dipper (*Cinclus mexicanus*), found bobbing in the creek; the violet-green swallow (*Tachycineta thalassina*), seen swooping between the canyon walls; and the canyon wren (*Catherpes mexicanus*), with a distinctive descending call.

## GETTING TO THE TRAILHEAD

The Havasu Trail is the only route into Havasu Canyon maintained for public use. The trailhead is 193 miles (311 km) from Grand Canyon Village by road. The Havasupai Indian Reservation, which borders the park, encompasses 294 square miles (762 sq. km) of rolling plateau and an intricate maze of cliffs. The trailhead is reached via I-40, exiting on U.S. Route 66 at Seligman or Kingman, and turning north seven miles (11 km) east of Peach Springs on Indian Route 18, a paved road leading sixty miles (97 km) to the parking lot and trailhead at Hualapai Hilltop. There are no facilities along this stretch, so travelers need to stock up on gas, food, and water before turning off Route 66.

Each of the following lettered sections corresponds to the letters indicated on the maps on pages 14–15 or 24–25.

Backpackers descending the trail in Hualapai Canyon

## ETIQUETTE

Visitors to Havasu Canyon are guests of the Havasupai people. This is their home. When outsiders take the time to make friends, they find the Havasupais to be a warm, generous people. The Havasupai Tribe asks reservation guests to follow a few basic rules:

- All visitors must obtain advance approval to enter the reservation from the Tourist Manager.
- Entry and camping fees are charged at the Tourist Office in the village where visitors must check in.
- Mechanized vehicles, including mountain bikes, are not allowed below Hualapai Hilltop.
- Hikers must stay on established trails.
- Visitors must keep the trail free of litter and pack out all trash.
- Hikers must give horses on the trail the right-of-way.
- Camping is allowed only in Havasu Campground.
- Cutting trees and shrubs is prohibited.
- Campfires are not allowed; campers must cook with gas stoves.
- Creek water must be purified before drinking.
- Liquor, drugs, weapons, pets, and nude swimming are not allowed.

*For camping, contact:*
Havasupai Tourist Enterprise
PO Box 160 • Supai, AZ 86435 • (928) 448-2141
touristoffice@havasupaitribe.com
http://www.havasupaitribe.com

*For lodging, contact:*
Havasupai Lodge
PO Box 159 • Supai, AZ 86435 • (928) 448-2111
lodge@havasupaitribe.com
http://www.havasupaitribe.com

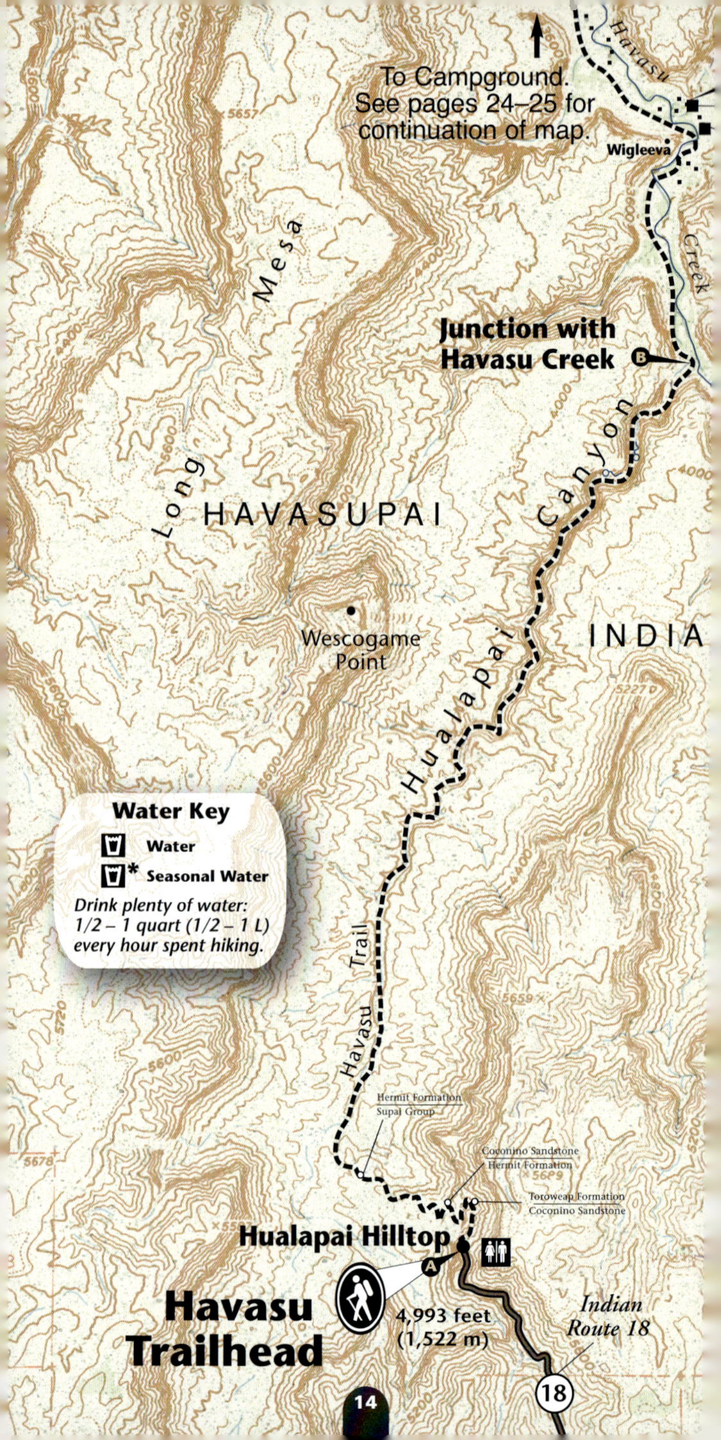

To Campground.
See pages 24–25 for continuation of map.
Havasu
Wigleeva
Creek
Long
Mesa
5657
Junction with Havasu Creek
B
Canyon
HAVASUPAI
INDIA
Wescogame Point
Hualapai
Havasu
Trail
Water Key
Water
Seasonal Water
Drink plenty of water: 1/2 – 1 quart (1/2 – 1 L) every hour spent hiking.
Hermit Formation
Supai Group
Coconino Sandstone
Hermit Formation
Toroweap Formation
Coconino Sandstone
Hualapai Hilltop
A
Havasu Trailhead
4,993 feet (1,522 m)
Indian Route 18
18

# Havasu Trail

## Hualapai Hilltop to Supai Village

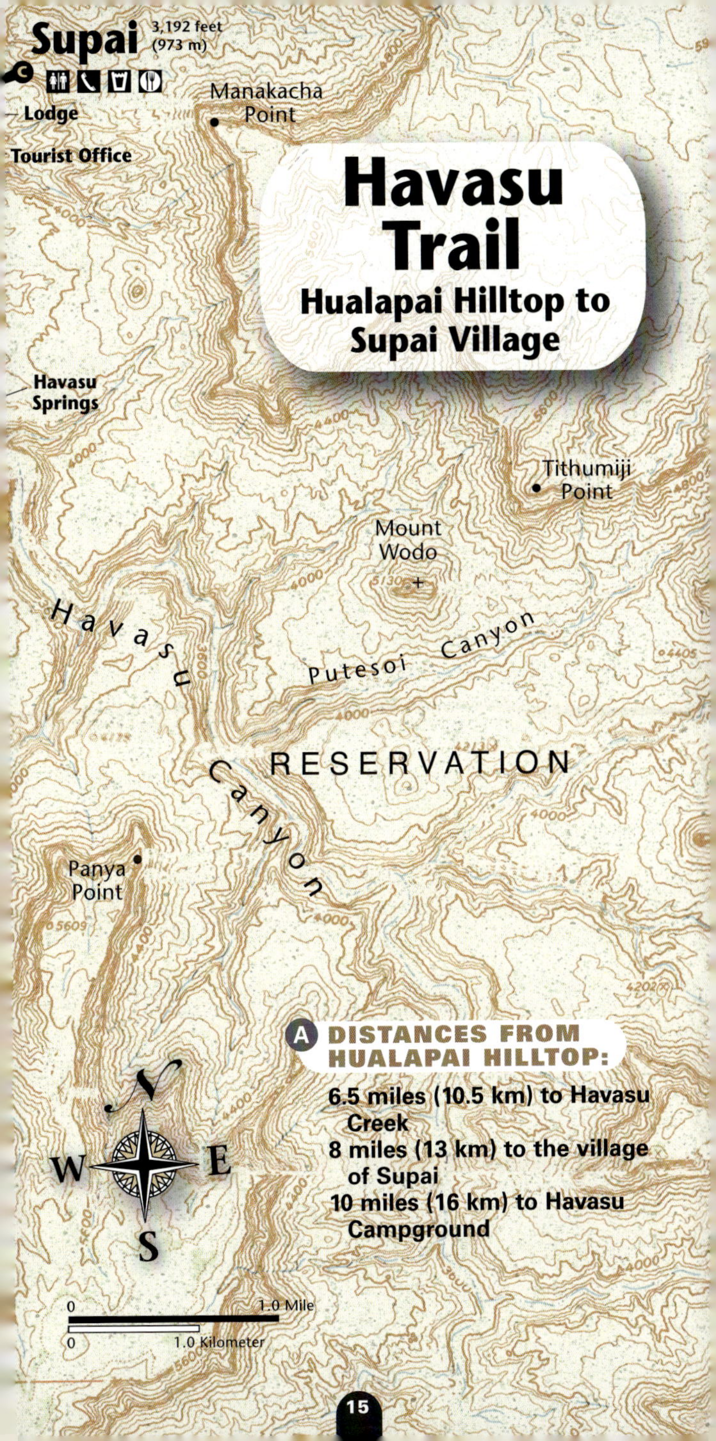


**A DISTANCES FROM HUALAPAI HILLTOP:**

**6.5 miles (10.5 km) to Havasu Creek**
**8 miles (13 km) to the village of Supai**
**10 miles (16 km) to Havasu Campground**

Horses, which carry supplies, tourists, and Havasupai guides, are a common sight along the trail.

## A HUALAPAI HILLTOP

From Hualapai Hilltop at an elevation of 5,200 feet (1,585 m), the trail descends a series of steep switchbacks through the Coconino Sandstone. Beneath the upper cliffs, the trail follows a long talus slope covering the underlying Hermit Formation. Although more than five hundred feet (150 m) thick, the Hermit siltstones and mudstones are usually buried under debris eroded from above. An inconspicuous plant called blackbrush (*Coleogyne ramosissima*) covers the slope wherever there is enough soil to take root.

As the trail descends, Mount Sinyella comes into view far down the canyon. Even at a distance it has a commanding presence. Older Havasupais warned outsiders not to approach it too closely. Mount Sinyella contained spirits that if disturbed might cause floods or strong winds that could blow people off the canyon walls.

Once on the canyon floor the trail winds over creekbed gravels, packed by the constant tromp of feet and hoofs. The trail becomes sandy where it leaves the wash for shortcuts across low terraces.

Occasionally, large boulders block the streambed at choke points, forcing the trail to detour.

Hualapai Canyon cuts deeper as it reaches the top of a major cliff-forming series of rocks called the Supai Group. The top member of this is the Esplanade Sandstone, whose rounded ledges look molded. The color of the cliff walls deepens to a dark red as the trail winds farther into the canyon.

Horse traffic on the trail may be heavy at times. Be alert for the sudden approach of galloping horses and be prepared to give them the right-of-way. Because no roads reach Supai, almost all of the needs of the canyon residents are supplied by horse. Supai has the last post office in the United States where the mail is delivered by pack train. For those living there, the mail means more than letters and bills. Groceries, clothes, and movies all arrive by pack train.

## B JUNCTION WITH HAVASU CREEK

The change at the junction of Hualapai Canyon and Havasu Canyon is dramatic. The dry desert suddenly transforms into a green oasis that borders the twisting course of Havasu Creek.

The trail reaches the creek, where it is screened by a thick growth of cottonwood, seep willow (*Baccharis salicifolia*), and arrowweed (*Pluchea sericea*). The sound of flowing water is heard before the creek comes into sight. It's like wind rustling the leaves. In Havasu Canyon living water is never far away. Even on a still day there is constant movement as the creek slips and eddies its way to the falls.

The tribe has posted a sign giving directions at the junction of the two canyons. This is the one critical turn on the trail. When you reach the junction go left (north) to reach Supai. If you miss the turn, a long, dry trek lies ahead.

In the August heat, 1975, a young woman and her dog went the wrong way instead of following the main trail to the village and campground. She quickly ran out of water and came close to dying before finding a tiny seep spring. It took her forty-five minutes to fill the only container she had: an eyeglass case. A Havasupai looking for strays spotted her tracks fifteen miles (24 km) up Cataract Canyon. He followed them into a side canyon and found her emaciated, but alive, twenty days after she made the wrong turn.

Havasu Creek rises from dry gravel a short distance above the junction. The springs that form the creek emerge slowly and quietly in little pools and rivulets. People often walk past them not realizing they mark the beginning of the creek. Within a short distance, the creek reaches full strength, flowing at thirty-eight million gallons (144 million liters) a day. The mysterious beauty of Havasu Creek is even more magnetic than other desert streams and has drawn people to Havasu Canyon for centuries.

Bright sunlight penetrates the water all the way to the sandy, mineral-coated bottom of the creek. The water, laden with calcium and magnesium carbonates, calcium sulfate, and magnesium chloride, forms a substance called travertine. The minerals are carried in solution until they meet the dry canyon air. Carbon dioxide evaporates, causing the carbonates to separate from the water and coating the stream bed with the light-colored travertine. The refraction of light entering the water charges the creek with shades of milky blue.

From the junction, the trail follows Havasu Creek, and soon the first signs of Havasupai farms appear. Irrigation ditches divert water into fields and pastures fenced with barbed wire. The canyon walls gradually spread apart, leaving a pocket of bottomland land one quarter mile (0.4 km) wide. People have lived and farmed here for at least 1,300 years. Eventually the trail leaves the creek and heads toward the village of Supai.

## C SUPAI

The first view of Supai comes at a rise in the trail. The village appears as an island of green sunk within an ocean of red rock. Where the canyon widens for several miles, about 200 acres (80 ha) are used as horse pastures or planted in crops and fruit trees. Two red pillars stand overlooking the village. These stone sentinels, called Wii Gl'iiva, are the guardian spirits of the Havasupai people. A legend says that if they should ever fall, the canyon walls will close and the village be destroyed.

When heading to Supai, turn *left* at this sign at the intersection of Hualapai and Havasu canyons.

Across the canyon from Wii Gl'iiva and directly above the village stand two other rock formations. One is shaped like a father carrying a child on his back. The other is the mother bringing up the rear. The legend of these rocks concerns the origin of the Havasupai people. When their ancestors began to outstrip the available resources in the canyon, the people split in two. One group decided to leave and travel east to find a new home. The man and woman regretted leaving. When they reached the top of the first cliff they looked back for one last time and were turned to stone.

As the trail enters the village, it widens into a sandy lane shaded by ancient cottonwood trees. This is Supai's main street. The road is just wide enough for two pack horses to pass.

At an elevation of 3,200 feet (975 m), Supai Village (so named in 1906 for its post office in the mistaken belief that "supai" was a Havasupai word) is the administrative and social center of the Havasupai tribe. A few older houses still stand, but most of the 500 residents live in newer, tribally built homes funded by government assistance.

Supai also has a modern lodge and a general store. Because of transportation costs, the price of food is double what it is on the outside. A cafe and the Tourist Office are located near the center of town. The tribe runs most businesses in the village and a school that goes through the eighth grade. The tribal council makes the major decisions affecting the tribe. It consists of a chair, vice chair, and five councilors, all directly elected.

Riders walk their horses along the dusty street, laundry flaps in the wind, and old men sit on benches in front of the post office/store and watch it all happen, entertained by the parade of backpackers passing through.

## D SUPAI TO HAVASU FALLS

Havasu Canyon widens dramatically as the trail leaves the village and passes the last homesite. In a half mile, the trail rises slightly as it rounds a bend in the cliff to reveal a panorama spanning nearly 100 million years of canyon geology. As you take in this view, consider that twice as much sedimentation once lay over the present-day rim. In the intervening 200 million years, these layers have eroded away as the Colorado Plateau rose nearly a mile above sea level. The erosion continues.

A sound of falling water filters through the trees ahead as the trail descends from the corner. In a short distance, a gully nearly seventy feet (20 m) deep and three hundred feet (90 m) across cuts all the way to limestone bedrock on the left.

At the gully's head, Havasu Creek used to cascade fifteen feet into an emerald pool where local children swam. Now the water plunges seventy feet into a rock moonscape. Two new falls punctuate the winding quarter mile before the creek gushes through a gap where Navajo Falls once dropped seventy-five feet into a chasm. Navajo Falls is no more.

This is the aftermath of a three-day flood in August 2008 that removed millions of cubic yards of pulverized rock and sediment at the foot of the Supai Monocline and deposited them in the campground below Havasu Falls. Everything bears the mark of the flood and subsequent repair work by the Havasupai tribe.

## E HAVASU FALLS

Havasu Creek continues cutting deeper as the canyon narrows. A half mile (0.8 km) farther the trail suddenly reaches the top of Havasu Falls, where the creek dashes through a notch worn in the travertine rim. The stream takes a tremendous leap into a luminous blue pool 100 feet (30 m) below.

A trail built by the Civilian Conservation Corps in the 1930s descends the left (west) side of Havasu Falls. Blue sky floats above the cascading white of the falls, which roar like a low-flying jet. Below the falls, curving travertine dams form a series of stepped pools.

A man walks across a levee that helps form the pool below Havasu Falls. The pool is a popular swimming hole.

Clear sheets of water slip smoothly over the rims.

Havasu Falls has changed dramatically since the turn of the twentieth century, when it was called Bridal Veil Falls. At that time, the creek spread across the brink in a lacy curtain, before a flood in 1910 channeled the fall into a broad fan and then in 2008 to the present spout.

After months of restoration, the pool below Havasu Falls now shimmers some eight feet below its 2008 level, still one of the world's most beautiful swimming holes. Resist the temptation to dive from the falls; few survive it.

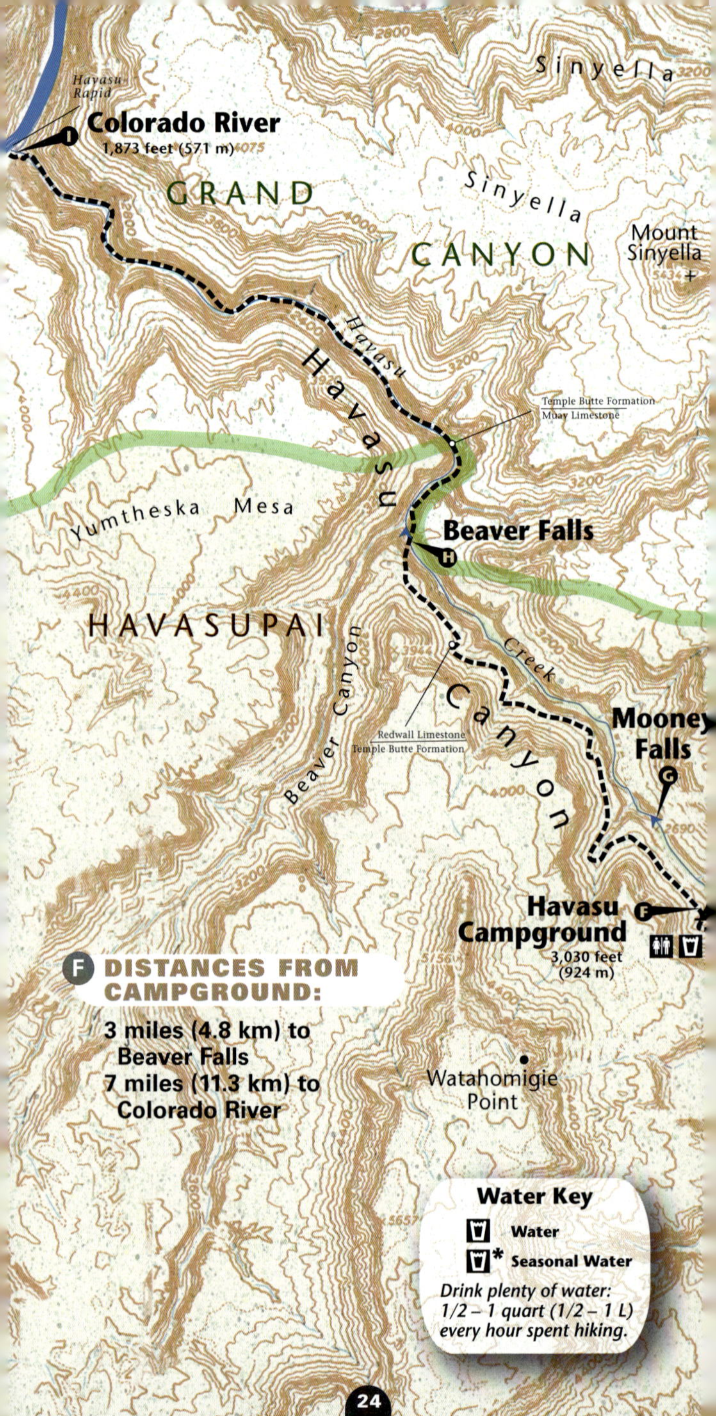
Havasu Rapid
Colorado River
1,873 feet (571 m)
GRAND
CANYON
Sinyella
Sinyella
Mount Sinyella
Havasu
Havasu
Temple Butte Formation
Muay Limestone
Yumtheska Mesa
Beaver Falls
HAVASUPAI
Beaver Canyon
Creek
Canyon
Redwall Limestone
Temple Butte Formation
Mooney Falls
Havasu Campground
3,030 feet
(924 m)
F DISTANCES FROM CAMPGROUND:
3 miles (4.8 km) to Beaver Falls
7 miles (11.3 km) to Colorado River
Watahomigie Point
Water Key
Water
* Seasonal Water
Drink plenty of water: 1/2 – 1 quart (1/2 – 1 L) every hour spent hiking.

Havasu Trail
Supai Village to Colorado River
Canyon
NATIONAL
Mesa
PARK
Towago Point
Ukwalla Point
NDIAN
RESERVATION
N
W
E
S
Havasu Falls
E
Carbonate Canyon
Supai Group
Redwall Limestone
Mulgullo Point
D
Supai to Havasu Falls
Schoolhouse Canyon
Supai
3,192 feet (973 m)
C
Lodge
Tourist Office
Manakacha Point
igleeva
To Hualapai Hilltop. See pages 14–15 for continuation of map.
0
1.0 Mile
0
1.0 Kilometer

## F HAVASU CAMPGROUND

Havasu Campground stretches along the banks of the creek to the top of Mooney Falls. Campsites are scattered in a grove of tall cottonwoods next to the creek, and when full the campground holds 300 people. Up until 1900, the Havasupai used the area to cremate their dead. The steep col behind the campground's Fern Spring was once called Ghost Canyon. By the turn of the twentieth century, under the influence of the Ghost Dance movement and pressure from Indian agents, the Havasupai began to bury the deceased; and the campground area no longer hosted cremations.

## G MOONEY FALLS

The creek moves placidly on the very brink of Mooney Falls just before leaping into space in a single 196-foot (60-m) drop. Higher than Niagara Falls, it is the tallest of the three major falls. Water explodes in pure, dazzling white as the falls hit a deep, green-blue pool.

The trail seems to end above Mooney Falls. But with care you can find the way below the falls by following an old miner's route. This begins on the left (west) and winds down the travertine rock, sometimes along narrow ledges. Two slanting tunnels have been blasted through the rock along the route. Steps are carved in the soft travertine and lead to a steep climb down to the canyon floor. This pitch is protected with chain railing and stanchions sunk in the rock in 2009 to replace the chain and drills originally placed in 1883. Waves of cool mist blow from the bottom of the falls, making the footing slick.

Mud-brown travertine deposits cover the cliff like falling water turned to stone. The color comes from iron oxides and coats of mud deposited by flash

**Mooney Falls plummets 196 feet (60 m) to an azure pool below.**

floods. Beneath the travertine deposits are wet niches where ferns, mosses, and columbines grow. In the shade of the cliff, swallows dart and whirl on the edge of the air churned by the crashing falls. Mooney Falls was the most sacred waterfall of the Havasupai. They called it the End Waterfall (Ha Gv'oma) until a tragic death gave it a new name.

In 1882 Alphonso Humphreys led a group of seven prospectors into Havasu Canyon to see if they could access claims below the highest falls. Young Dan Mooney, "a sailor tired of the sea," packed in a rope to descend the falls instead of risking the hair-raising crevice Havasupais used. Unfortunately, travertine fans on the way down probably sawed through his rope, and he fell to his death.

Eleven months later, in 1883, Alphonso's brother Mat created the route still in use today down Mooney Falls to look over the mining claim he had acquired from Alphonso and to bury Mooney's remains.

Ever since, the cascade has been known as Mooney Falls.

## H BEAVER FALLS

Between the main falls and the Colorado River lies a rich riparian wilderness. Tall cottonwoods and singleleaf ash trees line the blue water as it drops from one travertine pool to the next. A beaten path follows the creek, crossing terraces covered with fragrant canyon grape and passing under grapevine bowers.

The seven-mile (11.3 km) hike to the river takes a good half day and requires at least ten creek crossings. But there are really only two ways to go, the wet way and the wetter way, and after the first crossing the rest do not really matter. Because camping is not allowed below Mooney Falls, the roundtrip requires a full day. Be prepared for chest-deep wading, and remember that crossings are not always obvious.

Beaver Falls lies three miles (4.8 km) below the campground. You can reach it and return in a single morning, or take a leisurely day swimming at the falls or searching for the finest pools along the way. The reservation ends at Beaver Falls. From here down, the lower creek runs through Grand Canyon National Park.

To hike below Beaver Falls to the deep pools or to continue to the river requires climbing a bypass on the right (east). (Note that the trail can change dramatically in times of flooding and is best avoided when the creek is high.) The trail winds along the left bank of the creek as it reaches the top of Beaver Falls. Cross the creek and look for a route that climbs a travertine cliff to a high ledge above the falls. The climb is marked by a metal footprint mounted on a short post. To continue to the river, stay high until past the junction with Beaver Canyon on the left (west). From the ledge you have a good view of the falls-a couple hundred yards of cascades where the creek funnels through curving chutes and plunges into deep pools.

Havasu Creek cuts into the Temple Butte Formation at Beaver Falls. These thin beds of dolomite limestone are layered about 400 feet (122 m) thick. Below the Temple Butte lies the Tonto Group, but only the Muav Limestone is exposed. The Colorado River and Havasu Creek have yet to cut into older rocks in this area.

Below Mooney Falls, the trail crosses the creek many times.

Havasu Canyon near the confluence with the Colorado River